ON THE EDGE OF NO ANSWER

On the edge of no answer

Prose Poems

Joal Hetherington

BAUHAN PUBLISHING
PETERBOROUGH NEW HAMPSHIRE
2017

Library of Congress Cataloging-in-Publication Data
Names: Hetherington, Joal, author.
Title: On the edge of no answer : prose poems / Joal Hetherington.
Description: Peterborough. New Hampshire : Bauhan Publishing, 2017.
Identifiers: LCCN 2017010872 (print) | LCCN 2017010907 (ebook)
  | ISBN 9780872332386 (alk. paper) | ISBN 9780872332393 (ebook)
Classification: LCC PS3608.E852 A6 2017 (print) | LCC PS3608.E852
  (ebook) | DDC 811/.6--dc23
LC record available at https://lccn.loc.gov/2017010872

Book design by Kirsty Anderson
Cover design by Henry James
Cover art: *Folder of My Metaphors,* quilt made by Ludmila Uspenskaya

BAUHAN
PUBLISHING LLC
PO BOX 117 PETERBOROUGH NEW HAMPSHIRE 03458
603-567-4430
WWW.BAUHANPUBLISHING.COM
Follow us on Facebook and Twitter – @bauhanpub

MANUFACTURED IN THE UNITED STATES OF AMERICA

To my family and friends
who are at the heart of these words
and especially my mother
who would have been thrilled

To my poetry and writing peeps
who ushered these poems into the world
(you know who you are!)
and especially Mekeel
who made it happen

Contents

I / the little part of you that I know

II / plan b

III / whatever after

IV / compass

V / *guilty bystander*

VI / life in prism

this is the call you make to the phone that always rings

These are the numbers you know by heart, by finger memory, the way the pattern plays out on the keypad, so visceral that if you stop to think about it, it will escape you utterly. This is the outgoing unmelody beep by beep on your cell phone, the slightly different untune on your home phone that means the same thing. The phone is ringing now. This is the waiting feeling that grew up beside you. Have you ever been untwinned from anticipation? Which of you was born first? These are the questions you mean to ask. The phone is ringing now.

I / the little part of you that I know

lonesome

There was a lonesome in that house that retreated into corners when we came. Furred shadows. The winnow of voices flashing flashing flashing in the air. There were eyes half-closed in the neglected places, noticing the not-to-tell, not telling. We raised the dust, we breathed it in, sin-simple in the swearing by day. There was a listen in that house that fled to the attic when we came. Making winterdrift of cold, under-hum of summer swelling beneath the eaves. Floored and philandering, the footsteps coming that always meant going. There were closets coming into their own at night, nothing-scratch beneath beds. Miscellany rearranging its etcetera into metaphor. There was a lonesome in that house. There was a listen that came when we went.

things not said

This is a box. In it I am putting the things I am supposed to say, which will settle to the bottom as soon as I stop shaking it, heavier than the half-formed thoughts that come apart like dandelions and drift, impossible to reassemble, as soon as I touch them. The sides of the box are made of neglected thank-you notes and unreturned phone calls, lined with the beginnings of unsent letters. Amid the milky floating chaff are things I wish I had said, visual twitters of yellow and green as bright as chips of birdsong. The lid is a weave of unspoken regrets, clinging together with the barbed grip of Velcro. Will they be enough to seal it against second thoughts?

corduroy

You keep trying on your past: the name that says you without ever
quite being you, the places you've stood and sat and laughed made
foreign by frozen snapshots that yet arouse a flicker of what you once
felt. Here are the facts stiff as corduroy—birth date and graduations,
honors won and surgeries undergone, outlines of relationships inherited
and made and divorced—all carefully cut with pinking shears to keep
them from unraveling and stitched together through the bulky and
difficult seams. You've never quite stopped feeling like the shy child
in her homemade jumper, no matter how much the hard ridges have
softened and worn, shaping the fabric around you. Ah, but inside . . .
when fashion forgets you, when the closet door closes on the faux pas
that wear you . . . there's the seamless glide of moment into memory, the
thousand gleaming strands weaving and reweaving, as supple as living silk.

argument

Imprinted by argument, she carries the feel of it for hours afterward, acid-etched by the strain of assertion and anger. What led up to it seems more absence than cause, a mystery that stops short of the argument itself and cannot explain it. Nothing that preceded it bears any relation to the appalling sensation of having been altered to the edge of venom by her own fury, of there being no way back from the alchemical, abraded self she has now become. She feels with a visceral loss the words she flung away in the burn of the moment, feels them still unspooling into an irretrievable future. She wonders how he and she will recognize each other when they next meet.

the little part of you that I know

I call and ask to speak to the little part of you that I know. Three, four rings, on the edge of no answer, but then you pick up. This is not the voice I was expecting, formal and almost rosy, and I know right away, but I ask anyway. No, you say, that little part of you that I know is not there. No, you do not know when it will be back. I'm afraid I'll sound forlorn (that little part of you would understand), but there's no way to end this conversation gracefully—we are friends, after all, even if this is all pretext over subtext. How are you (without you)? What's the news (from the not-here)? Hanging up, I wonder—will you really bother to give my message to the little part of you that I know?

anger glasses

She is wearing her anger glasses today, her eyes pinpoint fierce behind the tinted lenses. The children know better. There is comfort among the coats and in the quiet wind lifting off pages they read behind the sofa or under the dining room table. Her staccato steps stalk the silence, reminding them of the knife of light that sometimes opens the door, reminding them to whisper clean across the stern floors. Up and down she goes, setting the kettle to shriek in the kitchen, the pipes to growl in the walls. Once the boy tried on the tiger-glasses and saw everything predator red and raging, the sofa fractured into a craziness with no comfort in it, the hallway narrowed into a tilt of defiance. Since then, he sometimes dreams in color: the anger glasses burning orange in a clear tumbler sitting on the counter in the pale bathroom, dozens of pairs of folded glasses dangling sulphur-yellow from the chandelier above the sanctuary at church.

Tic-tac-toe, the covert game the children scratch out in the hidden corner of the top bunk in their room, nearly always a stalemate. Click-tack-knock, the prowl of her passing the doorway, the hot whiff of her muttering on her way. In the pause, the girl's eyes are wide and still as the O's she has made on the paper. The boy looks at the girl without seeing, listening to the air in the hallway furring closed once more. He tries to imagine where she will finally put down the glasses. What color he will see this time.

isn't

It isn't what you said it was. It wasn't what you thought he did. It takes more than that to turn wine into water. It isn't whether, but when. It certainly isn't Zen. You might have got away with it if you'd known what it was, squandered without cause. What you didn't know then is the appendix to what you don't know now. It makes no difference—no matter how many times you count it, no change left over. It can't be helped, can't be hurtled, can't be hustled. It wasn't the final chapter, no amen. Nobody remembered when. It isn't pretty. It never was.

fortune-tellers

She didn't believe in fortune-tellers, except when she did. "You
have to try so-and-so," a friend would say, or her eyes would catch
on the promise of a sign, jarring her into a fresh awareness of how
wrong-footed she felt in the world, how what she wanted always
seemed to be somewhere else. And a hope that felt half like treachery
would impel her in to hear what the omens predicted. Even the least
convincing reading threaded glints of expectation into the hours that
followed; then there were the ones that made her feel seen, that sent
her walking through the world for days with the sense that her own
fortune was coming to meet her at any moment, hands outstretched.
The disappointment was a gradual, barely perceptible clenching back
into the narrow perplexity of the present.

niagara falls

They lean, curved as quotation marks curtailing all talk, on the rail, stunned at the turbulence surging past them. They had expected romance, the lace of the mist, the chosen thrill of spectacle sending its erotic pulse through their honeymoon. But this raw unregarding power dwarfs everything. His carefully rehearsed declaration—"I love you more than all the water that has ever gone over Niagara Falls"— is no more than a sour pebble in his mouth, more trivial than a lie beside the heedless plunge of it. Their future seems little more than a fluke to her, compared to the present pounding on just below her feet. They glance at each other, a recognition akin to terror, and clasp arms, leaning together above the insatiable falls.

"our friendship is a nebula"

—Mr. Penumbra's 24-Hour Bookstore, Robin Sloan

Our friendship is Silly Putty, capable of absorbing bizarre and random imprints and then kneading them into a seamless, increasingly smudgy whole.

Our friendship is a triangle, always requiring one other person to be complete.

Our friendship is a Maserati, an achievement of intricate machinery and a shared addiction to speed.

Our friendship is Leap Day, manifesting infrequently but with a sense of windfall gratification.

Our friendship is the G string of a violin, taut and capable of harmonics.

Our friendship is a letter waiting for a P.S.

Our friendship is a yellow rubber dinghy with bulging sides that make it equally hard to get in or get out.

game theory

You win. You lose. You lose. You lose again. Then you win. Each loss a conviction. Every win a promise redeemed in currency valid only here. Your opponents come and stay and go. Collections of features—cowboy hat, Medusa hair, green eyes, purple lipstick—provoking atavistic impulses that trump every logical question of who or what. You change your own avatar yet again, beguiled and appalled by the purity of your own desire to attract, intimidate, amuse. You win: your cartoon self grins and gloats. You lose: it fumes or all but cries. You lose. You win. You lose. Close your eyes: phantom wins and losses playing out in the ether. Earworm of a theme song repeating, siren lure calling someone you've never been. You lose. You win.

second person

You know who you are—the one who will read this in the shock of
recognition. The shock of being known. The words will be an arrow
that has chosen you—for grief or for delight, you are only beginning to
know, the way the flare of love obscures what is to come. Others will
close the book unscathed, but not you. This ink will be a tattoo that
you realize you already have, a pattern rising to the surface, left long ago
by piercings you thought had healed. A code invisible to others, indelible.
The turn of each page will be the opening of a door as you look for
the way in, again, again, the impossible way in to where you can at last
touch the hand outstretched to you, the warm and living hand on which
the ink is not yet dry.

promise of snow

I suppose I should have known better than to take an IOU from
anything as flighty as snow. But it seemed like such a safe bet, as sure
as night eating day, winter chasing autumn into the leafless woods. I
took out the carelessly scribbled promissory note the other day and
opened it: a blinding field of pure white, not a blemish of a letter on it
anywhere. It must have been written in disappearing ink—even when
I held it up to the sun, not a stroke was visible. But I haven't given
up hope that snow will remember, will redeem itself from its heedless
ways and come to annul the fray of every day, the desperate busyness
of sound and scurry that ravel the edges of everything without cease.
If I prop the promise in the window below the half-lowered shade and
stare, I can almost begin to see it.

descent

Each of his thoughts took a flight of stairs downward, subbasement below subbasement. There was something especially metaphorical about the way they descended into places he hadn't been, places with that damp concrete feel and unlighted smell that could never be dispelled by even hundred-watt bulbs. As they went down and down into unclaimed territory, he began to wonder if he might reach the center of the earth, or the center of himself, with the oppressive sense of something tiresomely momentous and appallingly predictable, for all that he'd never visited either spot.

shy girl

To speak and not be received. Quavering on a wavelength audible only to dogs and aliens, fever-pitch high and thin as mountain air. In every social moment her stillness is paved over by the clash and contusion of casual camaraderie, the traffic of everlasting exchange without any on-ramps. She is scenery, an ocean of meaning barely glanced at, a wave of prairie grass ruffling away from the wind of passing, a peak shrouded in cloud— until the shock of faces turning toward her opens a pause of bottomless expectation in which she must make herself plausible. The words go out: she sees each listener begin to shape them into the likeness they already know while the sound fleets away beyond all hearing bearing with it everything that is not a lie.

name

Every time she saw her neighbor, she waited for the name to come
back. She thought it might be Karen, but then she thought perhaps
the woman only reminded her of Karen from high school. Could it be
Lisa? She listened sometimes when friends were arriving next door or
the husband came home, but no one ever called the woman by name.
No one filled in the blank. The woman became a question, a qualm,
unmoored from identity, made more vivid by the fret of every encounter
that might expose this embarrassing gap. Names floated into her mind:
Bianca. Gretchen. Louise. Claire. Each one plausible in the first leap
of the idea, lending the woman a new aura of implication, before she
discarded it. She began to feel herself fixed in her own identity, while her
neighbor's gained facets and layers with every mistaken label, turning
her into a cast of thousands.

"do not liken yourself unto a rodent"
(advice from a friend)

You are not a hamster scrabbling obsessively in a whining wheel,
although some exercise might do you good. You are not even a hip-hop
hamster in target-bright clothes and a new roadster, just begging for
trouble in the desolate sepia landscape of a car commercial. You are not
a rat in a maze; no amaze for a rat following its quiver of nose around
corners—stand up. Your tales follow you, but how many betrayals can
be counted among them? You are not a beaver assiduously laying waste
to woods in search of praise and security, blunting your bite before it
consumes you. No matter how much you hoard, you can never outdo
a chipmunk for single-mindedness and swollen cheeks. Soft at the heart
of your bristle of doubt, when will you let your porcupine soul out?

thinking about money

"You are someone who thinks about money," he told her, the tone of his voice totaling something up, and in that instant she felt herself to be on the wrong side of the equation. She'd never thought of herself as someone who thought about money—she only cared about what it allowed her to do and how secure it made her feel—but once she started thinking about whether she thought that way, she was snared in a self-conscious loop that made her feel mercenary no matter what she did. That he broke up with her two days later seemed almost anti-consequential, as if the damage had preceded an accident, or news of a bequest had triggered the death that bestowed it. Counting over the loose change of her bitterness, compounding her dismay, she barely missed him.

tangent

It was all drift and drab, she says. They don't tell you about that—or maybe they do and you forget. She is speaking in my head, of course. Sometimes I try to listen to what direction her voice is coming from, what tangent it emerges from, so unquestioning that it must be coming from somewhere, these sound waves in the mind's ear. It was all grift and grab, she says, pleased at her own cleverness which is mine also. But her past tense pushes against my present. Will we ever agree about what's over?

waiting room

There is flint in the way she says no. A presumption of sparks that can't begin to overcome her metallic certainty. Something old-fashioned in the rigor of her spine that makes her floral jacket and tailored beige pants seem both frivolous and unquestionable. Beside her, the daughter is marshmallow soft in her desire to appease, conjuring suggestions—a glass of water, a magazine, a woven anecdote—with an infallible eagerness impervious to practice. She is a cheat, a chatter, a charlatan in the waiting room that draws itself in unforgiving lines about the Puritan figure of the mother.

dog

Every morning he calls the dog that won't come. The dog is in the
rosebush combing itself on thorns. The dog is tracing the tree map to
make sure that nothing has moved. The man calls again, as sharp as
any tyrant. Wanting what he wants, which in the dog's ears is duller
than the scrabble of gravel underfoot, more distant than the promise of
tonight's dinner. The man calls again—but look: he holds a coffee cup
in the world of both hands, quite full and still steaming. He has come
prepared for his ritual annoyance and in fact makes no move at all to
descend the weathered porch steps and give chase. The man calls again.
The dog is wriggling on its back in the grass, then scrambles to its feet
to follow a pungent scent toward the shed. The man lifts his face to the
sun and flares his nostrils, inhaling the scent of right now.

she's gone

It's not a song. It's the empty house with most of the furniture wrenched out as if by some catastrophe. It is a catastrophe, wrought and wreaking, the raw havoc before words. She's gone. It's mathematical, two overlapping sets drawing apart, less and less in common, until only the porous wall between them is still joined, the two bubbles elongating with the strain of remaining together. Whether they burst. Whether they don't. Neither will hold the house that held them, that told the happy ending first and added the conflict after.

how long

How long since the sun? How long since you thought you deserved the sun? How long since you felt the burn of it, simply sitting with eyes closed and letting it do all the work? How long since you measured how long before, three steps to the door? How long since the wind? How long since you just started walking without knowing where you were going? How long since you found out instead of in? How long has it been? How long since you let it win? How long since the birds, and how high was it then, remember when? How long were the days when summer was something and the walls were sky? How long can you lie?

calling

She kept her hand on the phone at night. The cool plastic casing was an anchor amid the tossed soft sheets, reassured her as she sank into the undulations of sleep. All the voices in her dreams seemed to come through the phone: Her mother calling to urge *Pick up the quarter, pick up the quarter,* and she looked down to see a wrack of coins glittering on the sidewalk about her feet. An unknown man calling from the driver's seat beside her to argue about the map she was holding. One night it was all wrong numbers and hang-ups, and she walked through the entire next day feeling mistaken and indignant. The alarm spoke to her in a different voice each morning, calling her back. And every morning when she woke, the phone was back on its charger or on a windowsill across the room, as mute as the day it was born.

you are

You are an eleven o'clock movie, too late to start but too tawdry to ignore. You are the anticipation of rain. You are the knowing smile of a passing stranger. You are a book with fourteen pages torn out in the penultimate chapter. You are a hyperlink lost in cyberspace, without the light metallic relief of an outdated robot companion. You are the mixed metaphor pointing two directions at once, a signpost rather than a destination. You are the sum of all your convictions and hopeful paroles. You are the very definition of someone else's hopes. You are the maddening meme of a song without beginning, end, or expiration. You are the midnight shadow on a sundial, all your urgency made myth.

II / plan b

plan b

It's only because plan a wasn't airtight that we're sitting here now, stuffing wads of paper into the holes in plan b. And since plan b is only a flimsier version of plan a, and the wind is picking up, you can guess where this is going to end. So why doesn't anyone ever come up with plan j, which couldn't help but be jubilant and judicious? Or the quixotic and quintessential plan q? Plan m, plan f, plan v—why, the possibilities are marvelous, fundamental, versatile! Begone, bland plan b! Think big! Besides, I'm running out of paper and it's starting to rain.

umbrella

Standing at the corner, she holds the umbrella like a question she refuses to ask. Clever and contrived, it arches overhead on its scaffold of metal spindles, a triumph of frailty inverted over the single leg it can never stand on. Depending on the dry assertion to hold it. There is no reason to trust the monkey faces gazing simultaneously down at her and up at the leaking sky from amid the rampant foliage of the printed design, but since the green fronds have not yet let any raindrops filter through, she does. She has not foreseen the wind that is about to lash the nonexistent sides of her portable bell jar into myth, the underwhelm the monkeys have been watching for surging from below to toss their jungle into wild abandon. The light changes. She steps off the curb, still shielding her conviction.

allergies

The word *extracurricular* always made him sneeze—something about
the clutter of syllables and the peppery edges of the hard *x* and *c*'s.
A prospective employer used it not once but twice in a job interview,
sending him into an epic sneezing fit; his attempted explanation of
the word's superfluity came across as contempt, and an offer was not
forthcoming. Other words waylaid him: The fastidious overtones of
disinclination made him flush a mottled beef red, head singing with the
same sense of shared shameful affront he felt when passing a homeless
man on the street. His fiancée broke off their engagement over the word
karma—she could not help feeling its rounded syllables in her mouth
like a weapon, knowing it made him break out in hives, and how could
she trust someone so at odds with fate?

the psychic downstairs

The psychic downstairs does not expect my rent check on the first. The psychic downstairs triple-locks her door every night but leaves it open all day, even when she steps out. The psychic downstairs would never dream of asking me to get rid of the cat I'm not supposed to have. The psychic downstairs never notices the trash until it's overflowing. The psychic downstairs can tell by a touch whether someone is sad; they are all sad. The psychic downstairs says her bad knees are a curse from her mother, who persists in her ill will even in the beyond. The psychic downstairs cups my hand, feathers her finger over my lifeline, and says "Long, long life" with regret in her voice.

home truths

The coffeemaker is bitter, longing for the bright taste of lemonade and summer. Beware the conspiracy of forks, should they ever overcome their divisions; they are united only in their contempt for those dreamers the spoons. All day the blinds await their unfurling, the chance to whisper secrets to the night unnoticed by the dwellers-in-light. The vacuum harbors explosive visions of anarchy and delights in growling out its frustrations. What can be said about the boxes in the basement? Mournful, craving the neglected stroke of attention, the unfolding recognition of the faith they keep. Mice covet the books, the taste of ink and education, covertly gnawing their way through words in search of portals into alternate universes.

deadline

She'd never met a deadline she couldn't miss. The threat of them unsettled her, made her feel there was an invisible blade poised somewhere above like a guillotine. But it was never clear just where the threat was—was the line itself dead, and why then would she want to rush to it? Was she doomed if she failed to execute her task with ruthless aplomb, and remained on this side of the line? Or was the freefall on the other side of the line the true danger, a desolation of extinction? She envisioned the deadline itself as a groove in the pavement where a heavy portcullis clattered down, trapping late-comers without, the besieged within, while she froze in an agony of indecision, wondering which way to run.

jeezum crows

The jeezum crows are perched on the fence, one, two, three, sooty and
waiting. Each time he invokes them—when connecting the wrong wire
to the terminal in an electrical outlet, or answering the phone to an
eardrum-thrumming voice, or contemplating the mess in the garage—
they hustle up their wings partway and caw an irregular commentary.
They look like crosses and sound like tin cans mourning what they've
given up. *Jeezum crows*, he says, tamping his foot over another hole left
in the lawn by a mole, and they fly down and begin to yank dandelions
near his feet with their shiny black beaks. They look at him sly-sidewise,
wanting to flap up to perch on his shoulders and head, but he doesn't
seem to see them, so they don't.

inside voice

Shhhh—inside voice, the mother admonishes her daughter, and the girl shocks still to listen. After a moment she can hear it, a blue-green surge shot through with a mystery of purple and cotton-candy pink, saying birdwonder and take and shine, as wide as asking. But when she looks up in astonishment, her mother has turned away and doesn't seem to hear it. *Shhh—inside voices,* scolds the teacher. *Now, who can tell me the answer?* And she turns her attention inward, listening to the irrepressible dark mutter of negotiation and flare and fling, but no mathematical conclusions are forthcoming. *Inside voice,* she thinks in the suffix and suffocation of night, when flashlight and book have been taken away, when the closed door refuses to speak, and hears the pliant ripples sound out from her touch, carrying ask in every direction, and waits for the echoes to come back.

the ghost in the typewriter

It didn't feel itself to be a ghost at all, and in fact was something quite different for which a name had not yet been invented or typed. It existed as a sort of energy, a palpable impulse embodied in the resistance built into the keys made to be flung by pressure against the platen. It had in it some essence of the typewriter's previous owner, her intentness and her modest oaths at mistakes, but far more the exigency of unbuilt words. The living waiting that it was wanted the press of fingertips, the symbiotic action of muscle and metal. Tracing the edges of the raised backward letters, it composed its thoughts, anticipating the next flurry of expression.

ouija

He knew even before the planchette trembled into movement what it
would spell: A-L-I-C-E. Like all true believers, Mrs. Abernathy had the
answer at her fingertips even as she asked. But he no more felt his late
wife in the room than he felt Elvis. What he sensed was far more alive
and troubling than the accepted ache of loss: the turbulent confluence of
energy from four sets of fingers that somehow sent the planchette scraping
and skating from letter to letter, making him feel possessed by the
upsurge of others' desires. Afterward, he could not exorcise the turbid
feeling of having been used, and began to avoid his companions of the
séance. They read his withdrawal as grief and denial. But he had begun
to realize that he was haunted by questions, not by Alice, a visitation
that could not be translated by the full stops of conjured answers.

camera

[Interior, night. An unnamed plateau. The camera pans across the landscape, seeking to create a panorama, but the light has not been cast. *Cut!* yells the implied director. *Cue the moon!* After some internal turmoil, a hint of light is invented. Interior, night. An unmanned plateau. The camera pans across the landscape as the curved edge of the orb rises above the horizon, quickly revealing itself to be a glowing, harvest-orange Q, reflected in the eye behind the lens. What seemed to be omnivorous shadow-trees resolve themselves into a grove of question marks posing as shepherds' crooks. *Cut!* yells the director. Everything pauses. *Did I ask for questions?* Interior, night, lit by a Q moon. An ungated plateau speckled with cloudy statements of sheep . . .]

substitute teacher

It's the call she hates most: from the School of Thought. Someone is out, out of fashion, perhaps moribund, and the only viable idea they can come up with is to call her. Just the thought of the labyrinthine hallways, their floors worn down inches below every classroom's threshold by the incessant back-and-forth, back-and-forth, not to mention the conflicting and complicated course schedules, makes her grit her teeth. And the children, with their young-old faces and the surprised petulance in their eyes when she makes them behave! If it's Metaphysics, she'll have to fight the urge to tether them to their desks to keep them from floating up to the ceiling where they pontificate at each other like leaking balloons. Even worse is presiding over the Mock Court of Public Opinion, where every last one of them wants to be the prosecuting attorney; it involves hours and hours of opinion polls, recorded commentary from TV experts, and rehashing of rumors, and no decision is ever definitive, seeing as how they all scramble behind the Mock Bench to sit in collective judgment, which is arrived at only because they've run out of time. The best part of this subbing gig is that no one really expects her to teach, no lesson plans, no grading. In fact, they probably choose her because of her reserve and hesitancy. It's occurred to her more than once that she is perhaps actually a substitute audience. She sighs, and hopes it will only be a day or two this time.

saint bernard

The dogs were one thing. Having a breed named after him was more pleasure than duty, a kind of pet responsibility that warmed more than demanded—although, of course, they were bred in service to travelers through the pass, whose welfare he guarded with the utmost seriousness amid the carnivorous cold. But the mountains . . . Becoming patron saint of the Alps opened in him a sense of crushing weight, of a stony despair so deep and slow-moving that it seemed rooted in time. The mountains leaned on him, shrouded in the icy mood of their own making, asking for incomprehensible blessings and intercessions. Asking for granite grace which would take the whole eternity of his faith to command.

insomnia

The jitter in your legs tells you there was someplace else you were supposed to be, but cannot tell you where. Somewhere in the heap of thoughts sifting, sifting through your mind is the one you didn't mean to throw away. Every toss is a you-turn, every turning-on of the light a blight: turn off, turn over, turn down. You are stubborn and sour, a scale playing itself badly, every jarring note tumbling you back down the half steps and whole steps to the beginning; you will never hear the end of it. You are the ghost of sleep, haunting yourself, palpable and recalcitrant among the ignorant dreamers. You cannot stop meaning yourself. You cannot forgive the day just past for what it didn't say.

carbon copy

This is the real story—the one with the blurred letters, the inky strikeovers of mistakes and changed intentions. No one could ever mistake it for its celebrity sibling out there in the world, unblemished and confident. The carbon copy has the same DNA writ fragile and flawed, its onionskin complexion unable to conceal a single thought. The least breath makes it flutter; it is not made to withstand strong criticism. Yet how stubbornly it persists, telling over its errors, preserving them against all reason, in the fade of its own obsolescence.

midnight dive

It's only night. It's the only night. Only night gives him this feeling, this suspension of belief. He can hardly believe he is standing here, suspended between airs, but belief has nothing to do with the spring and grit beneath his bare feet. Nothing to do with the gritty glint of stars overhead confusing themselves with the reflected glitter below. Below might be above, night rushing in his ears without a sound, filling his head with an ocean of space: when he leaps, he might just as easily dive straight up as down. How will he know? It's night after all. He flexes his shoulders, tests the visceral give of the board. How will he know it's night after all is done? Knowing has nothing to do with it. He tenses himself into a knot of night and springs.

april fools

She'd always wanted to meet an April fool; they sounded so much more intriguing than the common variety. They sounded so hopeful in their ridiculous faith in what springs, like multicolored lilies nodding their heads over a garden they reinvented simply by being there. They had a tensile green in them, April fools, the buoyancy of new unfolding, of something bobbing on waves. It seemed to her that the word *fool* had lost its currency, had become a clang in a bucket rather than the soft-starting spreading gong of sound it had been in Shakespeare. She wanted to believe still in the reverberating surprise of wisdom from unlikely places. All month, she searched the faces of people she passed on the street or met in stores, looking for the wide-open gaze of wonder or the sly, knowing delight. She listened for every question that had a yes built into it.

rattlesnake skeleton
(from a photo by Annie Leibovitz)

Who knew it was a feather, a fragile thing beneath sinew and muscle?
Gone the guard of skin, blood evaporated, and what's left is a coil of
old ivory spine and the slender articulations of dozens of curved ribs
housing air. Empty warnings at either end—the rattle still raised to offer
alarm, the diamond head reduced to a nub of its living intentions. Even
poison couldn't preserve its breath, the sinuous twine of flesh married
to the mercy of heat and cold. Even the taut spiral curving self into self
couldn't exclude chance. Only the delicate bone feather remains, hollow
plume of promise and threat.

parabola

He remembers when he was taller, the unearned sense of being looked up to, a rival to trees in the upright of his assumptions. He remembers the skyscraper madness of himself, the upward surge, when every new story existed not to be told but to be laid atop the others in the striving for altitude. The narrow self of the spine defied gravity, aiming for the omniscience of understanding. Even his fear of looking down from heights felt like a challenge to the status quo, a secret thrill of knowing he had higher mountains within him. He remembers being taller than the sheltering roof overhead, taller than the sunflowers and phlox. He remembers when he was taller than anyone ever knew.

wednesday's children

Why we? Why woe? Why wake us with weeping? Give flowers to
others and us the tears to water them? Where others see roses, we see
reckoning, daffodil dearth, loss in the lilies. Why make us the wild of
what would have been, aware and wasting, salt returning to earth?
Were we only the whether, the what-not on the way to someone else?
But we—we see both ways to smug Sunday, Monday fair with no ocean
to sail, Tuesday's grace not yet tethered by grief, the going of Thursday
that's only half a tide. Closest to solace, the unfelt touch of Friday's
hand, Saturday a surge of self-regarding toil. And unheeding Sunday,
oh spare the wail and spoil the blithe. Why think to shine on us now,
scape woe, sorrow crow, magnet of all melancholy? We are a well, a
weight, a wave folding endlessly into ourselves, knowing what you
only begin to guess.

the art of falling in fiction

It must be thoughtful. No pratfalls caught on camera, no tree root carelessly planted to waylay an unwitting chump. The art of falling is subtle. The signs are there—the rustle in the leaves on page 46 of something not yet startled from its hiding place in contagious alarm, the tearing sound of a decision on page 119 that weakens the fabric of everything to come—but only in retrospect should the reader look back and realize how inevitable it was. Don't overdo the weather. Let the words themselves make the sound of rain falling on the page. Darkness gathering in the gutters. Eroding the clean edges. And when at last you fall, as you have always been falling, it all comes with you, town and trees and conversations, all the woven thoughts ruched into an intention that can never catch or cushion you, and the reader trailing behind in the liquid folds of a silk scarf about to let go and dance on the wind.

III / *whatever after*

once upon a time, you were used to this

To the bed so short your feet crowd the end and your knees scuff the blankets up into mountains. To the sound of wooden doors closing down the hall and footsteps that never come any closer. To the dim pink air that breathes a kind of waiting to the one-eyed bear, the can palisaded with toothpicks, the book beneath the bed marked where you stopped with a gauzy doll's apron. If you slide a hand between the mattress and the bed frame, the flashlight will meet your fingers with its cold shine. If you slip the book from its stash and open it in your tent of light, you will begin to see. If you can remember the story. If you can read the words.

glass slippers

Once upon a time you ran barefoot in the grass, but that was before the slippers. Once upon a hearth you burrowed your toes through the feathery ash closer to the subtle embers, daring the line between comfort and flare, but that was before the slippers. Now there are always two ways about it, the smallest stain on your sole visible to multitudes. Now you walk on the possibility of shatter and shard every day. The sound of your steps is crystal; they sing in the piercing voices of angels when you walk in the rain. He is building you a palace of glass, entered by light in all directions. Glass nightingales will trill among a forest of transparent trees whose leaves tremble together in the tones of chandeliers. You will wear a dress of spun glass that remembers its molten history fleetingly where your skin touches it. How long will it be before you begin to see through yourself in your mirror?

ariadne

What an omen is a thread! Made of whispers laid parallel, spun into
something tensile, a belief made of next to nothing. It could have
broken in the labyrinth, snagged and sawn on a rough corner, but it
was made too well. It could have unspooled to a vacant end, but there
is no end to the faith we spin. I snatched it up as we fled to the ship, the
carelessly rewound reel that retrieved him, the only reminder of home I
took with me. I tied one end to the anchor chain as we left to come
ashore in Naxos, presentiment or promise? How easily it snapped
in the maze of the waves. Wasn't this where it was always leading me,
hanging by a thread?

"if there was a butterfly superhero, that would be him for sure"
—Jenny Grumbles on Storage Wars Texas

Here he comes! jinking and jiving as he approaches, distracted by
every bright flower, tussled by the wind. His wings are such a marvel,
especially when the rayed pattern is backlit by the sun, that those in
need often forget the agony of hitch and hesitation before he finally,
circuitously, arrives. If they've chosen their emergencies wisely, the
moment of climax will be reaching its mild height when he alights.
He is the man of silk and spin, reinventing himself in obscurity, able
to cross vast distances without expecting to return. One-way messages
are his specialty, as well as fanning overheated supplicants and distracting
crooks and small children long enough for the relevant authorities to step in.

how to tell time

No one knows what time looks like. Just ask your friends—even those who claim to be most familiar can't tell you; it turns out they've only ever caught a glimpse of him turning a corner as he walks away with that fluid, unstoppable stride—or he has left a room only moments before they entered it, a gasp of absence recognized infallibly by everyone who has ever been too late. They all agree that he is male, reason enough for you to doubt them. Death has a face, frozen in the implication of what was. The gods are resemblances by nature. But time is everything a pause is not, which is no reflection on you.

in the garden of mirrors

Perhaps you can be forgiven for thinking it's all about you—a rather tawdry misconception that says far more about you than any of the reflections you're so mis-taken with. The closer you look, the more fragmented you become, a glimpse in a tiny silver-bell, a glimmer in leaves of gilt, a glance off glass turning in the breeze, leaving you all edges at odds, as misassembled as a cubist portrait. But when were you ever faithful to your mirror, or it to you? Over your shoulder each one shows a light you never see, a labyrinth of refracted paths more vivid than the ways you ply by habit. The garden of mirrors makes chance out of light. It owes you nothing and will still be talking among itself long after you are gone.

waking

Each morning she woke bed-center in the heart of the world, a
pinpoint of warm, contracted awareness that swiftly expanded and
radiated outward, making things up as it went: the tussled feel of the
covers nested around her, the press of brilliant or cloud-fuddled light
against her eyelids, the cornered containment and daffodil yellow of
her room seeping into her even before she opened her eyes, the newly
invented tumble of shoes and books and half-played games revising the
roomscape of dresser and desk and lamp, her mother's voice rising in its
arc from inevitable to always there. *Rise and shine*—her mother's voice,
pushing open the door and snapping on the light by its very sound—
rise and shine. And she buried her head in the pillow, clinging not to
sleep but to that essence, that opening, that sense of creation in which
she was whole and new and unrepentant.

rearview (1)

She is putting on her makeup in the rearview mirror, as if intent on impressing someone from her recent past. Blush for nostalgia, eyeliner to give her 20-20 revision, mascara to flirt with what can't be changed. Last of all is the lipstick, a bing-cherry red perfect for blowing over-the-shoulder kisses. The slightly exaggerated image backcast by the mirror makes her look like a woman retrieved from a 1950s movie, the knowing type with an agenda that can only lead to trouble. Smoothing her hair behind her ears, she tosses the lipstick in her bag and puts the car in reverse, backing out directly into the fender-crunching path of a silver Mercedes.

rearview (2)

The tall brownstone and red-brick row houses glide past, a cavalcade
nearly overgrowing the street, their feet crowded with scrappy trees and
parked cars. She'd forgotten the past was so noisy. She'd forgotten
even while remembering that the past was so brash, shoulder to
shoulder without regard. The grit is no surprise, but the taste of it
suspended in this visceral surge of self-assertion takes her aback. Takes
her apart from her subsequent self. Glancing up, she meets the taxi
driver's eyes watching her in the rearview, watching her watch her past.
The jolt of it shocks through her like a glimpse of porn, making her
complicit, the voyeur of her own past, reminded that someone is always
watching, even in the city of her own self.

rearview (3)

She'd always hated sitting in the backseat—the occluded view, the way everything sliding past the side windows was already used and partial. The way, looking forward through the windshield, she couldn't avoid seeing herself looking back in the rearview, making her future seem like it was already happening without her and yet depressingly the same as the present. The almost-left-behind strain of carrying on conversations, forcing her voice to a speed faster than the car to be heard by those ahead in their turning away. She wished for the way-back of her childhood, the station wagon's sequestered backward-facing seat that opened the box of movement, let the stricture of passage flow out and widen into a plain of still-opening possibilities. The rear view that made a magic of where she'd been.

if I had wings, things would be different

People would look up to me. I would be bird-skittish, welcome among flocks of pigeons and clusters of sparrows, but fluttering from the human approach. When I landed and held out my hand, people would give me sandwiches, cookies. I would do my best to explain (from a distance) that I was no angel, no salvation, describing rooftops and cold perches in trees, dwelling in fallibility. With my own wings to catch me, I would overcome my acrophobia. Or maybe not, seeing how far there was to fall. Or maybe so, feeling the Icarus-flare of exhilaration, the soaring burst of release that makes the long exhale of gravity worth the after-all.

evidence of snow

The dictionary opens to snow. What kind of evidence this is he has yet
to determine; he examines the page carefully, the faint smudge beside
the word, the way it somehow stands out amid the hurly-burly of all
the earnest explanations surrounding it. The missing woman had often
been seen consulting this dictionary with a faintly furtive air by witnesses
who have now melted away, and the chill fan of air the pages made
falling open presaged his discovery. Was it foul play, a few random
flakes growing into a blizzard of malice, or merely foul weather? He
touches the cool page, seeking insight into where the body might be, if
there is one.

aloft

Once upon a time, a woman lived upstairs. Everything was there—no going downstairs to the kitchen for a cup of coffee, or to check that the sump pump was working in the basement. Near one corner of her home there was a door opening into a stairwell, but the steps that had once groped toward the ground had long since vanished, except for the very top one just below floor level. Occasionally the woman opened the door and looked at the lingering step with some confusion, as if to remind herself of something, then closed the door without looking any farther. In fact, there was nothing else to see below, since the lower stories had vanished as well, though the idea of them bolstered her sense of living aloft. Coming and going was a matter of faith. Sometimes simple intention was enough, and she would find herself walking down the brick walkway to the street she could see from her windows. At others, it took hours—once more than two days—before the idea of elsewhere captured her, solid enough to walk through. More and more the stunted single-story homes and the taller buildings with their blunt earthbound feet distressed her as she went about the town, and she left her upstairs less and less. One day when she hadn't been out for weeks, she realized she could no longer see even the closest neighbors' houses among the trees. The only voices she could conjure were those of the birds. Opening the pantry cupboard a little later, she realized things had begun to disappear—souvenir mugs from a forgotten trip, some small appliance whose mysterious function was outlined by its absence, the round blue canister of salt. She thought she would miss the smell and taste of coffee most of all.

midas's daughter

She remembers what it was like to be gold. The tumult of desire
suspended in its own answer, the slow atomic arc of time that made
striving irrelevant. Even in the instant of change, the impulse to move
diffused into a sense of the world so essential it resembled inertia.
She remembers the metallic feeling of being startlingly impervious yet
malleable, the golden haze through which the world chased itself at
breakneck speed across her vision. The deep cellular calm. And then it
was done, and she was snatched back to the heartbreak of breath, the
half-life of decay, breakable trust. Often now she sits in the restored
garden among the flowers distant with memories and waits for herself
to slow, listening for the eons-long beat of the gold lingering in the
heart of her.

prince

She began with Prince Charming and ended with a king. How different was the story then, the once made when. It was only in retrospect that she noticed how the handsome young adventurers in the stories were nearly always princes; even the sound of the word *prince* was carefree, a slip-slide away from responsibility, a swirl of dancing and dalliance. It was only after he succeeded to the throne—succeeded, as if what he garnered by default were another reckless achievement—that she saw what the stories glossed over in their rush to the end: how a king soon became a palisade, a stern determination, a rumor of war, the very sound of the word like sword striking stone. She took to hurrying past mirrors, not to see the sort of queen she was hardening into, the beat of her steps reassuring her of her own princess heart.

this is the kind of fairy tale

from which no one comes back. The kind that is left out of the celebrated collections, because how can there be a moral if no one wins? The kind that is seldom recounted because of the creeping chill it diffuses through teller and listener alike—and who after all has turned and returned to tell the untold tale? This is the kind of fairy tale that begins with a knock on a stump answered by a malevolent dwarf and ends with thorns, the kind in which the glittering stars turn out to be guttering candle flames caught in the tangled roots overhead in a vast cavern, the kind with no sky. This is the kind of fairy tale told by a crow feathered with the black marks of every error.

the god of karaoke

The god of karaoke has your number. It may take a while to find it, flipping through the thousands on thousands of cheat sheets, but when you do, you will feel known. Will feel spotlighted, in fact, by the panic of relentless attention that says *you*. The magnified microphone alarm awaiting your voice. But the words are given to you, *oh, love, put me down*, in all their awkward desire and plaintive kitsch, *met him on a train on Wednesday*, there's no hiding who you really are, lifted on the wave of music in the church of canned sound. The god of karaoke offers the soundtrack of excess, the crib sheet of catharsis, then listens as the faithful incandesce.

the goddess of silence

Who believes anymore in the goddess of silence? She is one of those outmoded into dusty mythology—just listen to the fractal clatter of today, the prohibitive thunder of monolithic gods; she is nowhere to be heard. But then, what could suit her more? Not even the rustle of offerings or the breath-wisps of prayer disturb her now. The unspoken is her pedestal; the hesitation within which thoughts flicker is her hearth. Unlike other faded deities who leave their attributes behind—war, love, dawn, fertility—she has taken the stillness she represents away with her to some unvoiced place that cannot be found by asking, that must be reimagined each time.

mermaid

She had a mermaid's sense of social niceties—curious and curiously detached. In the moment she was captivated by a conversation, an idea, entering it enthusiastically; yet once the immediacy of it waned, the exchange simply slid off and past her like water and as little regarded. Thank-you notes and returned calls were mere snags to be shrugged off, nowhere near as compelling as the present. From time to time she became enamored of someone and was possessed by an eagerness that took her out of herself and made her lungs hurt with the effort to breathe, to say shapes that she had no words for; only gradually did she slide back into her element and let the turbulence recede.

nixie

The water sprite could not understand how she'd come to be living in a post office. In fact, the present as a whole confused her, used to the rather baroque haziness of an etiolated mythology as she was. Some careless conjuring had summoned her (the dropping of an undeliverable package of Wiccan herbs and oils that had anointed the spoken curse words "Damn nixie"), and now she found herself stranded in this temple to paper. The dryness of it and the mechanical clatter of the sorters appalled her, and she withdrew among the pipes during the day or crouched in the dampness of the basement leaking longing for the river she'd been plucked from. In the night she began exploring her surroundings. The staff were only just becoming aware of her, discovering odd puddles on the floor where no water should be, finding more and more envelopes with the addresses water-streaked into indecipherability, as if someone had trailed her wet fingers across them.

whatever after

is what happens when the magic wears thin, when the invisible
hands of the support staff grow careless, beginning to leave streaks
of tarnish on the silver, letting the topiary animals in the gardens
grow into shaggy, ominous shapes crowding the paths. The prince
and princess notice, of course—not immediately, but soon enough
when lavish dishes arrive at the table tepid instead of hot and a torn
dress reappears with mismatched stitches that chafe the skin—but
they are helpless to wreak discipline among the invisible goings-on of
their acolytes. The wielders of strong spells whose whims brought them
here have grown old and are napping, or have set off (how long ago?)
into the forest in search of the magic herbs that have been so thoroughly
depleted hereabouts. The perplexed couple have begun to grow used
to unmade beds and vases of drooping flowers. The sly gardeners do
nothing about the briars beginning their slow, ordinary climb of the
castle walls.

coming back from the book

The cover closing like a door: Are you stepping into or out of a cliché? Everything in the room—chairs, lamps, TV, other books—seems to be watching you, wondering what this sudden stranger with the unfocused eyes will do. You miss the seen wind, realizing dimly how in this life it's visible only through the peripheral evidence of its thrashings and scatterings. The colors here are so much themselves, unmentioned and unmoving. You wait for your companion—the one you want to shake sense into, to kiss, to sublet your house to, the one as inevitable as a sister or a marriage—you wait for her to comment on the static scene, to set it glimmering. But her voice is turned away and receding: There she is on the caisson with all the other characters, a circus of arguments and anticipations rolling away toward the vanishing point, waving, waving, but not to you . . .

once . . .

Once upon a time there wasn't a man in an office on the 46th floor of
a 49-story building, and he wasn't wearing a blue-as-ice shirt open at
the neck with serious charcoal trousers, and he wasn't sitting with his
back to the window unable to see the pigeons swoop beadily by. And
he didn't see their shadows as omens of something about to fall on him,
and he wasn't waiting for the hard phone to ring. It wasn't Thursday
and it wasn't Monday, and he wasn't tipping a quarter from one
knuckle to the next with a gambler's smooth skill and he didn't have
pearly buttons on the cuffs of his butter-yellow shirt, and his assistant
was not sitting just beyond his office where the door could blink her out
at will. And he wasn't standing at the window of his 35th-floor office
looking into the arcane calculus of traffic skeining the street below,
and he wasn't thinking of how he had just seen her or how long it had
been or the bright and impatient way her face would greet him when
they met in an hour for lunch. And he wasn't waiting for the elevator to
fill in the blank before him, and he wasn't riding it up to the roof and
stepping off into the penthouse of the air, and he wasn't crossing the
vast compass pattern inlaid in the lobby's floor walking exactly south-
southeast, and he wasn't suspended in the endless moment just before
the phone didn't ring. And he wasn't wearing a sleek-dark raincoat or
a herringbone suit jacket, and he didn't wonder whether the morning's
unconvincing snow had melted. And he didn't have a blunt-nosed
gun stubbed under the bland folders in his brown alligator-textured
briefcase, and he didn't pause at the newsstand to leaf through the
Economist and *Playboy* with exactly the same attentiveness, and he
didn't need breath mints or hate chewing gum, and he wasn't sitting

in his executive desk chair leaning back back back with his feet on the sill and his face open to the sharp shard of sky framed overhead and he couldn't see his own reflection in the glass. And his shoes didn't need shining, and he wasn't craving a grandé latté, and he wasn't walking through the lucky-red doors of the House of Fortune into the steamy rice-and-brown-sauce smell, and he wasn't greeting her or shaking hands with his client or reaching into his glossy black briefcase. And didn't he mean it when he said he never missed her, or wasn't he lying when he said the project was on time, just fine, no problem? And he didn't and he wasn't. And once upon a time there wasn't a man in black pinstripe trousers and a stranglehold maroon tie standing at the edge of the train platform and standing at the edge of the train platform and standing in his blue suit and button-down ivory shirt and listening to the déjà vu of the train's demanding whistle and seeing with sharp distinction the difference between the step into blank air now before the approaching whistle and the exact same step ten seconds from now through the widening doors onto the floor whisked so neatly in front of him. And he wasn't riding homeward, and he wasn't sitting in his office working late, and he wasn't an outline in the air where nothing was happening at all.

IV / *compass*

railroad tracks

Along the railroad tracks, always a whiff of disrepute. Both sides of the tracks are the wrong side; it's the tracks themselves that make it so. The gleam of them all innuendo introducing thoughts not from 'round these parts, sly and suggestive. Along the railroad tracks, always the whiff of dispute. Always the train hurling in from afar, all brash and flare, making a fanfare of itself, turning the modesty of staying in one place into a mockery of the small-minded. Along the railroad tracks, always the whiff of things rethinking themselves. Grass raising its myriad heads. Plastic bags unburdened of convictions jinking and fleeting. Cinders not quite finished with their transgressions. Always the narrowing arrow pointing away from the wide-open illusion of here.

compass

There had never been a time when she wasn't dreaming of somewhere else. So often overlooked, even when she was consulted, she felt magnetized by the contrast between her impulses and her surroundings. She couldn't claim any special consistency: her emotional north shifted with her perspective, any away down an untrammeled road. When she moved, for college, then for work, it took some time for the familiar suspended tremble to assert itself in the chaos of the new, pointing away. Away was a vast place. She moved again. Never any closer, a sign rather than a solution, needle balanced on a fulcrum of old desire.

getting away with it

She knew someone who knew someone whose sister knew someone
who got away with it. Someone who played hooky and never got
tagged at home, whose scores on tests were always a little higher
than justified but never so high that they roused suspicion. Someone
whose smooth talk oiled the locks of doors both opening and closing
discreetly. Someone who knew people but was easy to forget. Someone
who flew above the birds but below the radar all the way to the
Cayman Islands, where the money still hasn't run out. Someone whose
golden tan is smooth and wrinkle-free, whose orderly cells divide like
clockwork, who is one step ahead of time, which hasn't even noticed.

fraud

Fraud is never flat. It wears a different face, mild as foothills when you don't yet see the mountains behind. Facetious, fickle, playing a game of favorites in which you only think you are the winner. Fraud is a flatterer, a fluster of understanding, a forever driving away down a one-way street. Fraud is always making new friends, forsaking the old to consternation. Fraud is a Ferris wheel glittering with lights, lifting fellow travelers to imagined heights, before they find themselves footbound once again as the fair closes. Fraud's every gesture is a Möbius strip, returning to where it began. Fraud is a fever of receiving, a furor of need, a fear of the future. With no other race to bet on, fraud must always finish first.

travel writer

Write about a place you've never been. Make it a color you've never seen. Add birds whose whistles sound like hair being dragged through a brush, and half-monkeys who can only be seen from the front and never from the back. These monkeys prove somewhat detrimental to tourism, since visitors can never be entirely sure that there isn't a monkey or two hiding in their overpriced hotel rooms. However, the resorts alleviate this problem by lining their accommodations with mirrors, guaranteeing that any potential monkey will be seen from some angle. The unintended result is that the island—it is an island, of course, suitably balmy and beach-fringed—gains a faintly blue reputation as a sexotic destination, much to the chagrin of its rather straitlaced inhabitants. They debate whether to close their borders to travel journalists, until they realize that someone will write about the place anyway, reinventing everything, and changing the color they've only just got used to.

good-bye

Good makes *bye* a promise, a wish of well. As if there were perfection in parting, and good-bye were a vow to practice until it's the best it can possibly be. But there is no best bye, no completely rounded division without return. And no one wishes enemies bad-bye, happy to see them leave town; even the riddance is good. Good-bye, we say, with the cadence of a closing door. And good-bye turns to gone by, yet another loose end for which you have no needle.

immigrant

Here are the furrows his feet are planting, hoping to take root. Nothing here knows the ways of growing familiar. Coarse leaves, controlled climate. The pendulum swing of one season to another is narrow, no room for the swoon of proliferation and ease that already begins to seem dreamlike, a conviction of home for him to be talked out of. Because of course that conviction was a barbed-wire tangle or he would not have left. Would not be here now, choosing the thorns for the rose. Forcing fruit as foreign as he to yield.

frequent flyer

All the travel contributed to the splintering of his marriage. Whitney grew suspicious—too many trips that didn't seem wholly justified—then accused him of having an affair. His denials changed nothing; when she calmed down, Whitney said that whether or not, it felt like infidelity, seeing him leave over and over. Her insight brought her into focus, made him regret their breakup. But he could not explain to her the unlocked feeling he got from flying, how his thoughts expanded and floated in unexpected directions, then wisped away to blankness as he landed. Each flight was part of an ongoing dialogue with himself, a train of thought— a flight of thought—he could recapture only in midair.

night road

A road at night. A ride at night. A risk made of metal announced by headlights. Hitchhiker under a sky of rivets, buffeted by the wide tidal rush of the wind through the prairie grass, empty and only. Coyote howl of a feeling. Then the car, and inside the hollow fleeing everything changes. Beyond the lit grass fleeting past on either side, everything must be invented. The road is black caramel, grainy and grasping. In the sonic glow of the dashboard, the thousand-mile sound of the radio answers its own questions, leaving the sidelong glance of the driver to its own devices. The car a needle, the road a suture, pretending to mend what has already been sundered.

state of grace

There is no police department in the state of grace. Any infractions take
place somewhere else—here one moment, gone the next, much to the
perpetrator's confusion. There are no speed limits needing enforcement
on the highways crossing the state of grace, and many who cross
it barely glance out the window before they're through it, fleeting
glimpses of something they think one day they might want to explore,
if there were any exits off the roadway. No chamber of commerce in
the state of grace, whose primary products barely survive barter and
immediately expire when sold. In fact, recruiting tends to have a reverse
effect, boomeranging the recruiter into the chaotic clamor surrounding
his intended target rather than vice versa. The state of grace is a place of
waving wheat fields, and musing mountains, and rearranging coastlines.
It has no major cities, and the population of its towns shifts constantly,
so that if you find them, their signs tell you nothing about who lives
there or even what they are called. News bulletins from the state of
grace are few and fragmentary; they come in Morse code, they are
overheard in rumors and snippets of conversation, they arrive in
wisps of song that linger in the memory like wishes, like tomorrows,
like maybes.

quetzal

Here, money perches on trees rather than grows on them. Feathered
the pungent green and red pulse of desire, it watches its watchers, takes
flight for tangled jungle reasons. Only other money can make it preen.
Here, money talks in aerials, song and squawk recorded by the land-
bound who learn, who lilt, who lure it with an acquired camaraderie.
Sometimes money cocks its head to listen, but their syntax is awkward,
the intended swoops of meaning farcical. It never fails to recognize
the unfeathered. Here, money ignores the needy, guarding only against
its true predators, owls and hawks with talons to spend, the kinkajou
greed that covets its eggs. Here, even the gods are named for money.

stony

Not for her the already uttered calm of sanded-smooth beaches. They drew her like tide to the ocean, they immersed her in a burning dream of yielding, all questions smoothed to a dumbness waiting to be over-written by footprints. But she could not stay there. Not for her the traded harbors with their ceaseless intercourse, their fathomed water mere underthought to the solipsism of commerce, although she could sit for hours watching, watching how the ships fanned out and dissolved into pinpricks in the vast jealous beyond. It was only when she found the craggy steeps and hard-fought pockets of beach on a northern shore that she felt she had come home. Coves where hard knobs and knots of black stone clutched the sand and argued with the tide. Ready assumptions wracked into spray even on calm days, threaded with the stink of seaweed. Places where things were far from finished, where the superfluous was no sooner spoken than scoured.

late transit

Rat on the tracks, the color of steel but disturbingly fluid, mercurial, first shock of movement as if the girders themselves were sending out feelers. Where there's one there is another in the yawn of no-train, and another. He feels himself to be in the gritty gawp of something alive and hostile, the cement underfoot rough as a tongue. He has put himself in the wrong, put himself in the way of night long past excuse, carrying home the gray nothing she will still expect him to say. Clang of the turnstile fleets the rats back to invisibility. The new passenger, young and alien, sits halfway down the platform, watching him from within a gray hoodie. Unblinking. The rats ooze back. Liquid steel beneath sleek pelts. He feels with shocking clarity the redness of his own blood, turbulent and shameful, the only color in this underworld of his choosing, fanned to flare by the first hot breath of the approaching train.

dearth

Everyone's a stranger on this dearth, this place where nothing grows. So many roots knotted underfoot, thrusting and tangling for a chance at air, but what overlies them is loom and not loam, overshadowing the shoots of effort. No one intends to come here—witness the looks of alarm and consternation on their faces, the way they cast back and forth like hunting dogs seeking the scent of their own vanished footsteps, the misleading paths by which they arrived. But that's never the way out. Like trying to walk through a mirror. Those with the best chance of seeing plenty again have the gleam of windows in their eyes. Beginning to gather flecks of fool's gold from the ground. Setting off through the mirage shimmer of distance into something else.

destination

—so you're plodding along, feeling ordinary, as ordinary as anybody ever was (weren't they?), one foot in front of the other, one word in front of another, wondering when on earth you'll ever get there, and if it's worth it, and even if there's a there there at all, and you start to have a suspicion you've been this way before, doesn't that park look familiar, doesn't that road-not-taken have a sense of déjà vu about it, haven't those people stopped their conversation over the fence at least once before to watch you go by, and how can you tell? and here's another corner or perhaps an old corner re-turned and all at once you're intersected by determination, seized by a spasm of inspiration, and you say to the man standing there, "I don't know which way to go"—not a question exactly, and not what you intended to say, but as close to the truth as you ordinarily come, and he says without pause as if he'd anticipated this, "Turn left at the next corner, then go straight for a spell and bear right at the oak tree. When you feel yourself begin to rise, close your eyes, turn in a circle twice, then walk backward, and you'll be there." "Thanks," you say, and turn the corner. You realize only after a few steps that you're now punctuating your run-on existence with periods. Like this one. So you keep walking, trying to feel how long "a spell" is, and wondering if you'll recognize the oak tree, and did he really say "oak tree," now you think about it you wonder if he said "smoke tree," and sure enough, after a spell (so that's what a spell feels like, you think) you pass a gray tree with a trunk of gritty smoke coiled impossibly and impermanently together and leaves of silver ash, and you keep walking, coughing a little, until your lungs feel hollow and your feet barely seem to touch the ground, and you remember at the last moment to close your eyes and pivot slowly with your arms outstretched, how can you tell when it's exactly twice when you have your eyes closed, but you trust and start to walk backward, and when you think it's time, you open your eyes and there you are at last, on the suspension-of-disbelief bridge, which has only a middle and no beginning or end, and you realize for the first time that all things are possible—

v / guilty bystander

do you really want to be news?

The sudden self exposed for what it really isn't? The fraction rather
than the whole, stark-lit by the blaze of attention that flattens three
dimensions into two? Do you want to be the object of envy, of pity, of
righteous anger, of admiration, of curiosity? How many shelves will you
be put on before this is through? Think of the uncountable clippings
you will be scissored into, the names of the folders in which you will be
filed. How do you reconcile yourself when you look at the screen and
see what everyone else sees? Will you meet that arrested snapshot self
on the street tomorrow? What will you say?

otherwise

How can she be otherwise when she is this-foolish, stuck in the shape
of every mistake? Otherwise is always the what-if. The smarter self who
knew to walk away, to choose that instead of this, that he was too good
to be true (another one looking for his otherwise, he too true to be
good). She is no wiser than other, standing here on the exact spot where
everything is real and without revision. The spot where doors slam and
alarm clocks ring and umbrellas are forgotten. The one place she will
never meet her otherwise. Sometimes she feels the roads snaking away
in every direction, tendrils of pathways along which otherwise is already
unfurling from the solitary moment. She imagines taking just one step
down one of these paths, then two, three, and turning to look back at
her fixed self, already a stranger, regarding her as she goes.

secret

It crouches in your mouth like a live thing. Inconvenient. Unpleasant, like the taste of fur. Each time you open your mouth to speak, it blinks and peers out, curious, sensing air and light, tensing in the gather of instinct—thwarted only by the catch-breath of your sudden recall. Sometimes it crowds your mouth like living cotton; sometimes it burrows beneath your tongue, as unforgiving as a grain of sand. Sometimes you nearly forget it's there, breathing in and out with you, a shadow almost identical to one of your own thoughts, until it nearly slips out, more by chance now than intention. The secret is growing older, less agile, less eager. Its time is coming—soon—and it has become aware that it will never matter so much to anyone again. You never thought you would miss the feel of it sleeping among your unspoken words.

tinfoil

His favors were like tinfoil—smooth and shiny as they unrolled, gleaming with goodwill—but they began to crumple at the merest dent and dint of use. The promised introduction, help building a fence, the offered ride—they covered what they had to but could only hold their shape against persistent need. There was a dull side to them that their recipients grew to know, and no smoothing out could ever erase the texture of creases and return the intention to its pristine state.

guilty bystander

It all happened before you got here. It happened when you weren't looking. What you know is like turning off the light and gradually, eventually, beginning to see the light leaking down the stairs from some dim lamp in a room above. There's a nevertheless about it as stringent as antiseptic. Which particular ignorance are you claiming? How can it be true darkness if you can see enough to recognize it? Most damning of all is that you're here, sniffing after the fact, implicated by proximity. When did you begin to know yourself as peripheral, and what are you still doing here?

on ice

Behind, the fringe of the shore arguing with the lake, insistence against indifference. Ahead, the blind expanse of ice, undulation smoothed into uncanny sameness, as if arrested motion and the air were made of the same color. She slides one foot forward, then the other, testing her grip, arms extended groping for the cushioning balance of the air. Walking on the ice feels like suddenly being in the spotlight, where every gesture is a risk of downfall, where all rehearsals fade into the critical scrutiny of the now. She shuffles forward without lifting her feet, gaining glibness, doesn't even flinch at the cracker-shot sound of the ice expanding farther out. The solid cold, more permeable than earth, is foreign underfoot, and with each step she becomes more aware of the vast fluid dark below it and how little she truly understands.

glib

Certain words skate across the surface of knowing: *glib*, like an oily feel on the tongue that glosses a hundred tastes into one; *cursory*, running at light speed across a screen, blanking what it ought to be taking in; *skim* hovering somewhere between steal and scurry. She finds herself in collusion with such words, hurried into decisions she hadn't intended to make, barely glimpsing interactions and intersections before she's past them. How buoyant the words are, gliding away without even excuses for luggage. No fixed addresses, no boxes in the basement, not a single photo album among them, while she, indicted, stands still at last, holding a photo of a boy in a lost wagon, awaiting the glib push down a cursory hill that never comes in the snag of a moment without explanation.

shadow

A man decided it was time to even the score against his cousin, who had repeatedly humiliated him in boyhood and whose brash, successful aura had continued to squeeze the man to the margins of attention in adulthood. So he prepared a special mailing box and began collecting doubts—no easy task, since they were so elusive, virtually invisible. The shadow of a doubt was what gave it away; one glimpse of a shadow and he would snatch at the air where it seemed to be, quickly perfecting his technique. Soon the box was full of his own doubts, with a few others' thrown in (although harvesting other people's doubts drew far too many alarmed looks and quirked eyebrows). Whenever he popped a new one into the box and slammed the top flap shut, he had the impression of things inside shifting, merging, separating, as if sometimes they fused into one amorphous whole and other times murmured by themselves. When the whispering of the box in the basement grew nearly unbearable, audible at night even from his second-floor bedroom, the man sealed it completely with packing tape, wrote his cousin's name and address in black marker (no return address), and took it to a post office in the city. It was surprisingly heavy, but the man gladly paid the postage. Returning home, he marveled at how still the house was. Though he never discovered exactly what effect his bequest had—his cousin died a few weeks later in a freak boating accident—the man had given away so many of his doubts that he didn't even wonder. His own shadow took years to recover.

the height of folly

Her parents named her Folly long before they knew how tall she would
be. Maybe it was the way her minute fists seemed to pummel the light;
certainly it had much to do with the reckless foolery that gleamed in
her face from the first days. By the time she entered grade school she
was a head above the other kids; by high school, she was six three. Yet
the kinds of teasing and outright cruelty that plagued other misfits slid
around her. Folly was nearly always to be found at the heart of some
quirky or misguided scheme that went awry; she channeled mischief
like a lightning rod, herself unscathed while the companions around her
were singed and jolted by consequences. Somehow they always forgave
her, seduced by the next twist away from the ordinary, the St. Elmo's
fire of faith that danced across her face each time.

cold case

You've been wondering for some time now just when you went missing, and no dogged young detective dedicated to sniffing out the truth has appeared on your horizon. One fact has emerged from your gauzy past: It's up to you. After all, you alone have access to all the bits and pieces—the incriminating evidence of your journals, undone items on old to-do lists (the crossings-out are harder to decipher), intimate knowledge of all the key players. Of course, they start to wonder when you turn up asking discomfiting questions with trick answers, and you begin to wonder whether it's because they'd never actually noticed you were missing or because they knew all along and kept it from you. You stitch this one's recollection to the edge of that one's anecdote, run your fingers along the selvage of another's certainty. The pastiche grows and grows without ever fitting together, and every hole between the pieces is the size and shape of you.

invaded by spring

Even before the opening of windows, the ants—large black ones in
twos, threes, sevens on the kitchen counter. Smackdowns. Ant baits.
Toxic spray. With each encounter, the living despair of groping toward
the long-awaited yet already building barriers against it. Evidence
of mice in the silverware drawer, spring-spawning, proliferating,
spurning the catch-and-release traps. Do or die, do and die, despiting
the makeshift hedges against the already happening. Silverfish. Smaller
ants in the bathroom. Awakening spider kingdoms. RSVPs pouring in to
invitations that were never sent out. Spring rave.

emerging from a comma

It was only when she drew a breath to continue that she became aware of it, the pause considering itself in which she had been suspended. That was always the way of it—the sense of in-knowing in the quantum between words that she never recognized until it was receding. Around her the world had urged itself along, only a little beyond, but enough to skew her sense of herself within it toward the cubist. So much rushing, crumpling itself around her like a fender reflecting fragments at different angles. And even as she felt this, her next words emerged, smoothing her back into the flow, weighted with a secret sorrow for all the commas dropping from text screens and run-on conversations and abbreviated feelings, vanishing into a vast calm understanding of invisible ink.

hospital

What she felt most of all was homeless. That this was not a place that would abide her for long, that she was in every way on sufferance here. The curtain of her pain was ruthlessly parted again and again by the antiseptic hands of those whose agenda she was. Rhythms at odds and imposed. The sounds of feet on linoleum and impermeable voices in the hall were as uncompromising as the surfaces surrounding her, hard plastic chairs and bland walls, metal skeletons of beds and sheets that verged on reproach. All of it a hurry, hurry not to overstay.

boy

The boy across the street stands in the yard again, shouting, "Maa-maa! Maa-maa! Maa-maa!" He doesn't realize yet that he is practicing not being answered, no tremolo of panic complicating the sound, all hot demand, a leash that he pulls and pulls knowing that she must come. Invisible within the fenced yard, he is only a voice, an arrogant exertion of need and expectation. "Maa-maa! Maa-maa!" And soon enough the door opens and her voice meshes with his, more often than not sharp and scolding, more often than not answered by wails and temper from him. The reassurance of the known rebuke. The answer that still always comes.

beside the point

You know the feeling—the cat staring at the empty air just beside you, all attention, and you realize that once again, you've just missed being relevant. Or your dinner companion distracted by something over your shoulder so that your conversation is now three-way, the subtext voice inaudible to your ears. There's no use in waving your hand, saying *hey*, stepping into the vacancy that isn't—it only highlights the truth that you're here and not there, that you're playing catch-up, with all the desperation that implies. Yes, now you see what the point was. Now you hear the third voice in your head, saying *Wake up, wake up, it's late.*

jumper (1)

Witnesses said they saw him looking over the rail. Witnesses said they saw him jump. Dark-haired man in a green shirt and jeans. Man who left his bike behind. What they said and what they saw were not the same, witness being withoutness, no matter how inner the moment of seeing seemed to them. Seeing, they could not be him. Could not tell the police his name or which salt grain of anguish pushed him at last to the edge, could not say when he lost his mother or his job, could not point to where in the river his stubborn body flowed, refusing to be found. Could not recount the flying fracture of falling. The splinter of knowing each witness carried away could not be extracted, could not be made whole, no matter how many days, weeks they watched the papers for news of a body yielded at last, a name that could never tell them any more than the unknown shaped by the scattered shards of their seeing.

jumper (2)

He opened the river like a book he would never be able to read. All the despair of knowing shattered on impact with the first indecipherable lines. Terrible words filled his lungs and surged before his eyes, fluid and utterly foreign, erasing the ordinary story of doubt in the crushing atomrush of change. Hesitation expelled with breath. Irretrievable. No lightness in any ending the river might write. He closed the river like a book you will never be able to finish.

undone

She made mandalas out of not finishing anything—always the
incompletion marring the perfection of becoming. A chore left undone.
A project stretching out of shape past its deadline, the peeved client
on the phone, the built-in rebuke in her head. An intention half-
constructed, aged from bright burst to mournful nostalgia each time she
revisited it, an image of what would not be. What was not completed
could not truly be destroyed or judged. What was not finished held its
particular place, a specific self-contained sphere that fenced out the
wide, perilous question of what would come next. Occasionally she
became aware of the flaw in this reflexive thinking, the unfinished gap
through which the world blew in, through which the multicolored
grains of sand streamed out into the unknown, and was lifted for one
comprehensive moment to the edge of elated, terrified abandon.

ticket

Even in her dream there is no free parking. She has come back from
some place of harbor (where?), trudging the long blocks through the
snowy dark, through the early (how far?), to the place she abandoned
the car last night in the blizzard (how long ago? how long is snow?). In
the starting of the engine there is assertion. In the flare of the headlights
there is the assumption of morning. The brushing away of snow from
the dome of roof and sheer of windows is its own satisfaction. And
then he is there on the other side of the car leaning in the open driver's
door, and the welcome of help she feels is stabbed through with the
realization that he is writing her a ticket. Why? she asks, the only word
that emerges from her crowded throat (why must you do this?) (what
for? can't you see that I'm trying, that I'm leaving?). I decide these
things on a case-by-case basis, he says, never looking at her. Why?
she says again, a twist of anguish. He frowns, still writing. If only the
mothers were here . . . he says.

walk-on

Here, between commas, is your cameo. Slightly cinematic, but nowhere near as dramatic as you'd expected, commendatory but, let's face it, rather common. No exclamation point. No run-on sentence. Something more for Mom's album than for tomorrow's tomes. Maybe you could do more—a come-on in a come-hither camisole to command attention, bells clamoring in the campanile, a cross-country caper in a red Camaro—but that would smack of complicity or overcompensating. You could complain, but to whom? And what is there really to recommend you?

porous

She started to notice everything she had thought was hers turning up in
other places. One day in a secondhand bookstore, she saw two obscure
titles nearly side by side that were identical to two she had on her own
shelves; a shock of panic sent her leafing through them to make sure
her name wasn't concealed in the gutter or some other obscure place,
as was her wont. But even the stroke of reassurance of touching her
own copies at home that evening couldn't allay the sense of betrayal by
a renegade self. A few days later, she read in a novel about a character
who wrote his name in the gutters of borrowed books, and began to feel
borrowed herself, an old plot getting older. The dresser she'd reminded
herself to dust only the day before turned up in a storage locker on a TV
show; in the detergent commercial that followed, the hapless husband's
technique of folding clothes might have been her own, the evidence in
her own drawers. In the subway, she glanced up from the palisade of
her book straight into the face of her mother—the round puffy cheeks
and slightly stubbed nose, the overly permed frizz of hair—worn by a
Chinese woman whose distant gaze excluded her utterly. The shock and
rattle of the double loss inhabited her for days. Then the long-gone fruit
plates glimpsed in someone's kitchen, the yip of her first dog heard in
a crowd, a familiar-looking old postcard in a bin at a flea market that
proved to have been sent by her brother from a family vacation to a
friend half a continent away—she felt herself dissolving into the world,
the boundaries of every feeling growing porous.

ignorance

Oh, be ignorant! Let the unread newspapers go joyously to the dump
to spread their tidings among potato peels and paint cans. No need to
reiterate scribbled messages or review the exercises on old school papers:
the grade remains the same. Cereal boxes with their tidbits of nutritional
advice, flyers promising enlightenment by subscription, phone books
with their outdated populations—close your ears, let them demand
attention from each other. After all, in this age of recycling, they're never
wholly gone, simply morphed into some other field for expression while
their electronic counterparts clamor in vast swarms on the Internet.
After all, you can never really embrace unknowing, you with your hoard
of books and half-written beliefs: you simply choose your ignorance,
keeping this, not that, even now barely admitting the relief of letting
your contract with omniscience lapse.

VI / life in prism

irreducible

That is where you wish to be. You learn to let go of things—pages, the husks of what you once wore, albums and archives, the dishes brought to you by hunger—with the gesture of opening hands that crosses from lofting to waving. Your thoughts grow lighter and more fleeting, less likely to return. You seek the space within embrace, the place where love lets go without conjugating regret, a universe within an atom— so near and yet . . . No matter how much you relinquish, something is always changing, something coming, something growing into the bloom of loss. You give up the work of hands, but the hands remain. You wish to be irreducible, but the wish is one too many.

with different eyes, what would I have seen?

Clarity instead of cloudiness? The numbers crisply outlined and fixed to the blackboard, instead of moving mysteriously in my mind to find their places? Would I have understood the expressions on my playmates' faces and been nimble enough to negotiate them? All those blurred mornings groping out of slumber, all those ritual relinquishings of hard edges on the way to sleep—contacts out, glasses off—would the shock of instant definition have altered my outlook? Conviction instead of caution? The betrayal of my weak vision was believing in *eye see* rather than *I see*. These are the seeing of me, the eyes I will be buried with.

more the same than ever

The sense of being smaller within the same space. Not shorter
exactly, but more doll-like, as if there is no hope now of stretching up
and touching the ceiling. But there was. The sense of being less elastic,
of the space itself having grown old around her. Sometimes she becomes
aware of it while standing at the sink looking out the window, looking
into the well of light that grows deeper every year as the trees yearn and
lean above the yard; she feels flattened, compacted, as if the windows
themselves were growing while she merely grew into herself, more the
same than ever.

peepers

Listen to the peepers saying *You are not alone, you are not alone.* The song they learn from cold mud and cold blood, wired to the edges of night and spring. These are the first thoughts in the wild shrill of themselves, the heedless here of something just begun. And every one is the beginning of a chorus. Cold water, cold breath, there is no daytime translation of this, these slivers of sound streaking the dark. *You are not alone, you are not alone.* Relieved of the swollen self-regarding light, the questions emerge as answers, every *where* a *here* in a darkness that is never complete. *You are not alone—*

the story is outside you

You bounce it like a ball, the big reddish rubber kind you remember from grade-school games, distracted by the gratifying *boing* it makes on pavement. *Boing, boing.* Seized by impulse, you throw it at someone, but the person dodges with the instinctive ease of long practice and the story rolls away, bobbling over the coarse grass into some shrubs. Terrified of losing it, you scramble after and retrieve it from its nest. But it feels different now, lighter—is this really your story? You toss it in the air experimentally, then again, stepping forward to catch it, and become absorbed in keeping it aloft as you walk, catch and toss, catch-and-toss all in one motion now. It *is* lighter, pausing in midair, hovering before it descends, until you toss it again and it barely hesitates before floating away into the woods. Panicked, you give chase, stumbling deeper among the trees while your story seems to negotiate the crowding limbs with ease, jinking and rising, gaining on you, receding into a pinpoint of color and breath before it vanishes completely. And all at once upon a time you look around and see where you are, lost and controvertible, inside the story you have yet to tell.

the end

THE END, the story says. Declarative. A simple period isn't enough—
think of all the other periods that have made endings that aren't, always
more letters to follow. This one, it would have you believe, is different.
No escaping, only white space thereafter. THE END. Such concern with
closure—the story almost never declares THE BEGINNING, and there are
no signposts through THE MIDDLE. But should you emerge from the
thicket of words, scratched and disheveled, stepping up to the cliff that
falls away offering the El Dorado of a sheer panorama, there stands
the story with its sign, THE END, asking to be taken at face value.
Asking you to believe that intention stops here, that the afterlife is a
figment of pagination.

holding still

It only works if you think of it as flying—soaring, hovering in place, the
kind of vivid unmotion that achieves a state of grace. Otherwise it's an
endless stop-action of failed effort, the muscles that twitch, the refused
world-worrying itch, the blink that shutters the day into a frame-by-
frame shatter. There is no stopping for the living—only the balance
of the motion you're always in, atom spin, lift of breath, drift of time,
your reckless earthbound fling through space that not even death will
end, that you can just—begin—to feel if you hold the singing soaring
moment—quite—still.

origami

She spends her time making birds out of words. Folded wings, sharp creases of beaks. The smudges of letters making mottled patterns and feather strokes. On sunny days she carries her paper pigeons out to the deck and scatters them about her feet. She sits watching with her coffee, and soon enough the wind begins to lift them, at first just a stir, then a startle as their meanings catch the air and rise, taking off. When they are gone, she makes more—never enough birdwords in the world. Some days she strews sunflower seeds on the deck, hoping to see some of them alight once more, searching for a glimpse amid the rustle of the greedy paper squirrels.

horizon (1)

Sorrow is a horizon. She can see all the way to it, but it keeps its distance—a little hazy and indistinct just where it meets the sky. A long way of birds and unfettered wind. The long way of phone calls that still reach their destinations. These are the prairie days that mimic childhood, so wide and burning, so plausible, but now she sees not the overturned bowl of the sky but the cradle of the earth. Not the beckon of beyond, but the abeyance of swaying golden fields, the close reading of the green garden. Every evening the far haze diffuses upward as the sun sets, blurring all careful distinctions. Each night, knowing clasps its fingers loosely about the house. But morning returns the horizon to its place. She can see all the way to where sorrow begins.

horizon (2)

Sorrow is a horizon, as near as the ocean, as far as an imagined shore.
Close in, the everlasting reminder of middles, of motion without
beginnings or endings. On blue days the seam between sea and sky is
a hard line, decisive as the stroke of sudden grief seen from a distance.
On gray days the clouds loom down in tendrils and threads seeking to
weave water and air into one, a veil that draws the inevitable closer.
Remembering how sound carries over water, she counts her words like
shells, like stones, keeping them for the time when they will be sent
skipping toward sorrow as it comes to meet her.

lily-of-the-valley

Make these words small as lily-of-the-valley. Let them grow in the woods close to the ground, green blades of return gathered against the long forgetting. Make these words the tiniest of questions, answering themselves always in white. Leave the colors for the crowded feelings, the upthrust and burst to the uncompromising. Let these words be fragile bells that sound without ringing. Let them listen. Make these words small as lily-of-the-valley. Give them the essence only found by looking, the potent surprise distilled by sorrow. Let them last only as long as that, grace gone to ground, fragrance as fleeting as the haunt of you in my mind.

gravity

Half of rain is gravity. Do you think of the miles of rain overhead, the sheer distance each drop has traveled only to end here? Do you consider how forgiving rain is, when nearly anything else dropped from such a height would kill you on impact? Tears, however, are only three-sixteenths gravity. A handful of rain, a handful of tears—feel the difference. Rain will not rest until it finds bottom, an almost magnetic pull. Tears have the flyaway buoyancy of salt, willful strife, striving toward somewhere else.

doortown

The rain is always news, but who listens? In this town they talk about
it before it comes, they talk about it in inches after the fact, but when
the rain speaks up, driving rushing scattering down the streets, they all
hustle in behind the doors and do their best to ignore it. Look for the
places without doors where you can let the inscrutable sound wash over
you—the box of a bus shelter in front of the bank, a dugout carved into
the red clay edging the high school baseball field, the abandoned lean-to
overlooking the meadow down in the woods whose weathered gray
planks drink in the rainlight like soft silver. Listen, but don't expect to
understand. Where do you go from here? All roads lead to driveways
and doors, except the ones that lead to more roads. Which door will
you open first?

walk me out

Walk me out of the sour of myself, out of the paper-white brittle of being made word. Wake me out of syntax without wind. There is the door panel-painted white; why describe the brass handle when you can feel the cold hard of it, the blue open? Swivel me into the swirl of updraft and sidewind, sand-driven to a shoreline where other unmoored things scavenge up, unravel of seaweed, unhinge unhabit of shell, inkblur of letters lost at sea. Whistle me out of the stoic and starved, the staved and stunted; whirl me into weather and wane, the wonder of how it never fails to come to this.

do you?

Do you curl like a wood shaving released from the lathe, or like an alarmed hedgehog? Do you close the book because you're done, or because you can't bear to see how it turns out? When you beat a retreat, do you play timpani or snare drums? Do you look for landmarks or larks? Do you choose the cracked cup because of its character, or because you're saving the best for later? Do you turn on the light thinking bright or dark? When you weather the wild, are you water or wind? Do you store your memories in cardboard or in tin? When you scatter the ashes over the sea, does your heart go with them or stay here?

life in prism

You have been sentenced to life in prism. Hereafter you will be part of
a crowd, meeting each and every other aslant. The light will find you
wherever you are in the most oblique ways, and you will always see
more than one aspect of any issue. Whatever you do will be reflected
back at you mercilessly multiplied from all angles. Sometimes you
will find yourself in a blaze of revelation, folded and refracted into an
excruciating complexity of awareness, scintillation without parole,
drawing lines between divine and doom. There is no escape—but
remember, like light, you will find your way out in all directions.

a-

I am a drift of atom and intention, directional and temporary. I am
a wake, backwash thinking, watching over what's gone past. I am a
sleep that sounds the steep, plumb-line deep. I am a thwart of every
expectation, a miss marking mileage with one eye on the mirror. I am
a loft out of labor, shuttlecock shot and shy of sky. I am a ware and a
warning with a mind of weather. I am an other, no mother, all feather
and fleeting. I am barely a pace from this very moment, a part in the
curtains veiling the crowd. I am a slant, sun-sliding sidewise, a ray of
slope. I am a rival without portfolio, a wry reckoning of what's owed,
a bode of better. I am a maze of whether and whiff, primordial as-if
turning knotwise and nether, a cord of occasion, a cost, a claim, a
sunder of sorrow, searching for a door.